the unfolded notes…

Richard Clark Gierman
-r.c.g

the unfolded notes

Instagram/Twitter: @richardgierman
Email: **richardgierman@yahoo.com**

First Edition
ISBN: 9781792745836

the unfolded notes

these are the notes that have come to me
when i forced myself to revisit past pain and reprocess those
situations

i sit back into the pain
and this has become my outlet

seemingly the only way to get my point across
in a way that is heard

i hope you find glimpses of hope and
are able to connect with the text on these bland pages

i do not specify who these are written about

some are of

past relationships
friends
God
life
trauma

i hope you enjoy them and find an outlet that gives you freedom

these are the unfolding of those notes that i have held close to me

thanks,
-r.c.g

i always saw you.
even when you felt alone
there i was

r.c.g

i still find myself smiling at the thought of us
the endless possibilities of what could've been

r.c.g

i may have never told you
but i thought you would be the one to stay

r.c.g

it kills me that i view you as a stranger now
when you were once all that i knew

r.c.g

all the world will see how much you mean to me
the darkness that was once inside of my head
vanishes as you walk in to the room

r.c.g

i loved you in a reckless fashion

r.c.g

the smell of autumn is thick in the air
i've told myself i wouldn't come here again
the pain inside pulls me back each time

i am overtaken
at the smell of the earth that plagues my mind
with memories both good and bad
flashes of the hell that i've endured

i hate the chains that bind me to this place
i am shackled down by the memories
engraved into the being of who i am

r.c.g

pieces of you
show up at audacious times

r.c.g

no one ever told me that
i could not undo what we had

r.c.g

i am so thankful that God
has allowed us to exist
in the same timeframe

r.c.g

you make me feel like i have a home

a distant feeling
that i don't think i've ever known

r.c.g

you were broken glass
and i cut myself
trying to hold you together

r.c.g

like wild flowers blooming out from the concrete
you came through
in a beautiful fashion

r.c.g

we are like the moon and the sun
chasing each other around
and once we finally meet in an eclipse
everyone stops and stares
but quickly
we carry on

r.c.g

Your presence swept in like the wind
in a moment
i am overtaken by You

r.c.g

i saw a glimpse of you today
in the face of a total stranger
i saw the light i once saw in your eyes
for a moment
you were on my side again

r.c.g

no other fire will compare
to the one i felt
when i was with you

r.c.g

i have felt many things
i am not sure that love
has ever been one of them

r.c.g

i have never felt a touch as powerful as yours
days after you're gone
and you're still imprinted in to every part of me

r.c.g

the unfolded notes

the history between us is not for the story books
i don't want there to be a past tense of what we were

r.c.g

the void you left me with
has been unable to be filled

i long for the day that i can trust someone
like that again

r.c.g

our shadows used to run wild together
now even they are lonely

r.c.g

your eyes tell me that you have already moved on
i am hanging on with everything i have
i know that it is still not enough for you to stay
but here i am
and there you go

r.c.g

no answer was given.
alone and confused.
after time you learn to live without someone
now I'm finally free

r.c.g

the unfolded notes

i have had to unbind-myself
from the person you made me think i was

r.c.g

our broken hearts only know pain

the pieces of someone else's broken heart

can it fill the part of mine that you took with you

who can fill in that space

r.c.g

our eyes have yet to meet
but somehow
our souls are already intertwined

r.c.g

the unfolded notes

the rain fell heavy on the night
that you shattered my innocence

the smell of moisture in the air
used to repulse me

for years
i have dreaded the weather that took me back to that night in a
parking lot where you felt entitled to a body that wasn't your own

the million times i said "no"
still wasn't enough for you to believe that
i actually meant no

i have learned to make new memories in the rain
so that i can focus on those
instead of what was done to me

i am still learning...

r.c.g

i was a burning fire

you had gas in one hand
and water in the other

you chose to put me out

i wish you would've fuelled me instead

r.c.g

we spend so much of our lives
trying to get someone else to love us
when we do not even love our self

r.c.g

you came through and broke down all of my walls
the walls that you begged me to let go of

then you were the very reason the walls grew higher

r.c.g

to be with You
even in complete silence
is enough

r.c.g

the unfolded notes

we were like autumn leaves

beautiful
but slowly dying

r.c.g

your heart is far too beautiful
for the hell it has absorbed

r.c.g

i decided to chose you
and you weren't even mine

r.c.g

the unfolded notes

i am scared to know what true love is

i have only ever been hurt before

is this the only kind of love i will ever know

a love that leaves

r.c.g

the unfolded notes

my heart sunk at that terrifying moment

when i knew you would go

your words fell void
and you were gone

r.c.g

you made me feel like glass
both fragile and delicate
but also transparent

you somehow saw deep inside of me
and you chose to shatter me

r.c.g

i look up at the moon
and think of you

maybe
wherever you're at
you look up too

and in a different life
we're together again

r.c.g

the unfolded notes

i sunk into you
then you made me believe
i couldn't swim

r.c.g

like the sea

i stood on the shore
and you pulled me in

r.c.g

sometimes the hardest thing
for us to feel is worthy of love

r.c.g

the unfolded notes

i hope the moment will come

i will come downstairs to you in the kitchen
stop before i enter the room
and gaze at what i thought i could never have

you will be the one who stays

r.c.g

the unfolded notes

i miss reaching into the backseat
of the car searching for your hand

the moment your hand met mine
nothing else mattered

r.c.g

i remember watching
your hair blow in the wind
as you sang along to all the songs
we loved together

r.c.g

i pray that no one makes you feel the level of isolation i felt after you left
a piece of me went with you

r.c.g

i am tired of trying to forget you

you made it clear to me
that I was forgotten
long before
you ever left

r.c.g

the unfolded notes

my mind silently screams for you
in the most quiet of times

r.c.g

the unfolded notes

forgetting you was harder
than i thought it could ever be

i had to push out the memories of you
that were so deeply engraved into my mind

the chains that grounded me to you have been broken

r.c.g

the unfolded notes

i know what we were
was so different in my head

r.c.g

i never thought a day would come
where I could wake up
and not wonder
where you are

years later
i am thankful for the hell i had to endure
you have made moving on easier

r.c.g

the unfolded notes

you noticed the storm behind my own eyes

i let you in

r.c.g

the unfolded notes

i attached myself to the wrong person for years

each passing day a part of them died

in time
we are all set free

r.c.g

the unfolded notes

you asked about the things inside of my head
and you listened

r.c.g

i have realized that sometimes home
is not an actual place
but a feeling

r.c.g

you know that feeling
when you were a teenager
and you felt like nothing could get any better than this

that was how you made me feel

but we all had to grow up at sometime

r.c.g

i long to know
if i am holding on to the memory of you
or if the memory is holding on to me

r.c.g

the unfolded notes

i spent so long in the darkness after you left
that i forgot what the sunlight felt like

r.c.g

my heart craves for another person
to come along and make me believe
i can truly go on

r.c.g

the unfolded notes

i hate knowing that you are completely fine
while i sit here in the aftermath
of what has happened
trying to pick up pieces of myself along the way

r.c.g

the unfolded notes

i smile when I think about the future of you + me

r.c.g

i am not where i want to be

the vast space between here and there
holds endless opportunities.

r.c.g

the unfolded notes

i hid for so long

only to find out that no one was seeking

r.c.g

the unfolded notes

i saw a light in you that very few have ever seen

r.c.g

the unfolded notes

you were the closest thing to safe
that i have ever felt

i never wanted it to leave

r.c.g

i would give almost anything
to be taken back to the moment
when I saw the same fire in your eyes
that i had in mine all along

r.c.g

the unfolded notes

we are all stuck breathing the same air
trying to navigate life

r.c.g

the saddest feeling in the world
is knowing that you are being only half loved
and yet you still choose to stay

r.c.g

i looked into the future
and all i saw
was you by my side

r.c.g

i find you

in the chill breeze from an open door
in the sunset
in the smell of a bonfire
in the laughter from a stranger
in the moon when it's half shaped

there you are

r.c.g

the unfolded notes

there is a space in my rib cage
that has been repeatedly misused

the fragile outline of where a heart once was

r.c.g

a lonely heart
in search of someone else
who is like me

r.c.g

your absence left me no option but to survive
i grew to know that you
were never what i needed

r.c.g

in a room full of shattered mirrors
i could barely make out my own reflection
i let my identity be manipulated by others

r.c.g

the temporary moment we had will stay with me
i wish i had known this

before
i was stuck with forever

r.c.g

the unfolded notes

the way you looked at me
had me thinking that i was present

for once
i felt found

r.c.g

the unfolded notes

i felt it in my soul
i knew when you left it would hurt

i saw you slipping all along

i watched you retract all the words you spoke
that gave me life

r.c.g

the unfolded notes

you were like a chill autumn breeze

i felt you so strongly for a moment

and then you were gone

r.c.g

the unfolded notes

one day
i woke up
and you were suddenly rendered powerless

r.c.g

i never meant for my words
to cut you this deep

r.c.g

the thing about pain is that it belongs to you
it is yours
and you feel it

r.c.g

if i knew one day
i would have to say goodbye
i would've withheld my hello

r.c.g

the unfolded notes

you forced me to live a life divided

life before you
& after you

r.c.g

maybe our hearts collided
but just at the wrong time
can we go back and try this again

please

r.c.g

the unfolded notes

i keep letting myself fall into
the hands of those who only crush me

r.c.g

my arms will always be a place you can run to
when everything else is confusing

r.c.g

the unfolded notes

these hands that once held yours
are now empty

r.c.g

the unfolded notes

i have moved on

but in the smallest way

pieces of you find your way back to me

r.c.g

my biggest regret is holding on to those
that have let me go long before i did them

r.c.g

on cloudy days
where the beams of sunlight are rare

i think of you

i wonder what parts of your world
i make an appearance in

r.c.g

the unfolded notes

i hope you never get put through
the same pain that I was forced to feel

without permission
it overtook me

r.c.g

the unfolded notes

in the quietest moments

your voice still resonates as the loudest one
in my head

r.c.g

the unfolded notes

i believed the lie that it would be different this time

i allowed myself to be entangled
in your mess all over again

r.c.g

the unfolded notes

it used to hurt
to remember you

r.c.g

the unfolded notes

i was left to live in the absence of you
our memories provided me with warmth

r.c.g

the unfolded notes

remind yourself

that you are worthy of being loved

i am learning to do the same

r.c.g

sometimes

you have to let go of the people who do not value you
so that you can know your worth

r.c.g

i noticed something about you…

you only ever wanted me
when you did not like yourself
i was your muse
i allowed you to treat me like a doormat
coming and going as you pleased

r.c.g

i still find myself searching for your face
in a crowded room
hoping for the chance that your eyes meet mine

r.c.g

you came through with a match
and burnt down everything that i built

r.c.g

i held on to you so tight
hoping it would be enough to make you stay

perhaps that is where my first mistake was

r.c.g

the saddest part of our story
is that after all that time

we are strangers again

r.c.g

2am
slow dancing in the kitchen
you+me

r.c.g

the unfolded notes

i burnt myself by letting you continue to damage me

r.c.g

the hardest part about being the funny one
is that no one ever sees when you are truly hurting

r.c.g

we carry around these wounds that few will ever know about
the tracings of those who have hurt us

r.c.g

no one ever really teaches us how to move on
they just keep saying that one day it will get better
it makes no sense to me
but they are right

r.c.g

the unfolded notes

i crave Your presence in my loneliest of times

r.c.g

the unfolded notes

you made me notice the rain racing across the windshield
i learned to appreciate the smallest things

r.c.g

i do not like the way our play has ended
can we start over again

r.c.g

i run from people now

it is what happens when you are hurt
by those who have claimed to love you

r.c.g

i know i will never be an easy person to love
i care too much
i ask too many questions
my loyalty is often abused by those closest to me
i worry that the one i love will leave
and i act irrational when i feel people starting to drift away

r.c.g

i was a lost and wandering soul

i was simply existing

but not living

the days were gloomy

light seemed so far away

You came and saved me

You have forever changed me

Your way is better

r.c.g

the unfolded notes

the air that is left in my lungs still has a story to tell

r.c.g

the unfolded notes

i know one day the greatest story i will tell will be ours
you are there in the waiting
hold on for me
i am in the waiting also

r.c.g

the unfolded notes

i want to make a place that we can bury each others wounds in

r.c.g

the day i met you felt familiar
like i had been there before
in front of you
in awe of you

r.c.g

the unfolded notes

i worry that i am too much for some
that i am hard to handle and be around

at one point i decided to stop caring
i was done hiding myself from others

r.c.g

the unfolded notes

i wonder how you tell your version of our story

r.c.g

i never knew that when i lost you
that i was also losing a part of myself

r.c.g

sometimes it feels as if i have been trying to catch my breath
for my entire life

r.c.g

you do not need to rush your healing
sometimes it is ok to sit and just be broken
you can have strength within your weakness

r.c.g

my heart was hidden behind locked doors and cages
all it needed was you to unlock it

r.c.g

if you shouted inside of my heart
your name would be what it echoes back

r.c.g

i laid my true self on the floor before you
a sight that is rarely witnessed by others

r.c.g

i don't know why my mind does that
takes me back to the person that you were

not who you are now

r.c.g

your name is no longer the one i scribble
on fogged mirrors and windows anymore

r.c.g

Made in the USA
San Bernardino, CA
06 January 2019